How To Write Bar Exam MEE Essays

Alexander Marcus

D. Randolph Adams Press

10 9 8 7 6 5 4 3 2 1

ISBN: 979-8-9875337-0-3

DEDICATION

To my mother

CONTENTS

ACKNOWLEDGMENTS

Thank you to Loren Metzger-Marcus, John Young,
Steven Pine, Susannah Tobin, Susannah Kroeber, and Laura
Kaiser for reading various drafts of this manuscript and
for providing immeasurable amounts of
helpful advice and suggestions.

INTRODUCTION:
THE DIFFICULTY WITH MEE ESSAYS, AND THE RIGHT WAY TO APPROACH STUDYING FOR THEM

> **SUMMARY**: Learning how to write bar exam essays is tough because the process is often treated as an offshoot of learning the legal material rather than a topic unto itself. Therefore, it is helpful to begin with an open book, and to peek at the legal rules, so that you can learn the mechanics of essay writing as a process distinct from memorizing the underlying legal material.

DISCUSSION: Essays on the Multistate Essay Examination (MEE) portion of the bar exam test two things simultaneously:

(1) your knowledge of the legal rules being tested.

(2) your ability to craft a coherent, well-written essay by applying these legal rules to the fact pattern that you have been given.

What makes the process of learning to write MEE essays tricky is that, at first, it seems like you cannot become good at step (2) until you are already decent at step (1). In other words, it feels like you need to first memorize the rules – which overlaps with your preparation for the multiple-choice Multistate Bar Examination (MBE) – before you can become fluent at writing essays.

This order of operations is a problem because learning the legal rules is an incredibly difficult and time-consuming task. Practically speaking, it means you do not get a chance to work on the nuances of MEE essay writing until mere weeks before the bar exam. For instance, when I studied for the July bar exam, I felt uncomfortable with my essays all through June and up to about the 4th of July. This was because it was only then, with three weeks to go, that I finally felt comfortable with the underlying legal material, and progressed to step (2). In retrospect, I wish I had found a way to prepare the nuts and bolts of essay writing long before I had most of the legal rules memorized.

The difficulty in learning how to write MEE essays is that bar exam review courses are primarily focused on teaching you the MBE material. However, this orientation is often suboptimal for learning how to write MEE essays. From their outset, most courses give you a steady stream of essays to write. You are told that you will struggle in the beginning, but you should try your best, and you should not worry if you need to look at the answers. While this approach reduces the stress caused by repeatedly writing poor essays, it does not make your essays any better. Fortunately, there is a better strategy, as detailed in this guide.

The key to learning how to write MEE essays is to separate step (1) (knowledge of the legal rules) from step (2) (essay organization and rules application). You must begin to learn the nuts and bolts of MEE essay writing long before you have the rules memorized. Here is the simplest way to do so:

> *(i) Whenever you struggle with an essay,* **<u>stop</u>**.

> *(ii)* **<u>Look up the legal rules</u>** *in question to refresh your memory. However, be sure not to look at the rest of the model answer.*

> *(iii)* **<u>Now, with the rule in front of you, try again to write the essay</u>**.

This process will simulate what it will be like when you have the rules memorized. It will also help you to cultivate the ability to write a thorough, well-organized essay in just 30 minutes.

With this approach, a lack of knowledge of the legal rules is no longer an obstacle. You can learn how to write MEE essays long before you have mastered any underlying legal material. You will know what it feels like to organize an essay properly, without needing to wait until a few weeks before the bar exam for all the pieces of the puzzle to come together.

This guide is a concise tutorial on writing consistently high-scoring MEE essays. It is not a text covering the underlying legal material. For that, you should enroll in a bar exam review course. Rather, this guide is a supplement designed to help you accelerate the process of learning to write MEE essays.

The key to writing a successful essay is to make sure that you dissociate the mechanics of essay writing from memorizing the legal rules you need to know. This way, a lack of knowledge does not inhibit mastery of the essay basics.

Parts 1-5 of this guide go through the basics of a well-written essay. Next, Part 6 presents a simplified, two-question mock MEE. Finally, Part 7 applies the methods of Parts 1-5 to the mock examination, providing sample "excellent" and "fair" responses for each essay, as well as a detailed discussion of what makes the "fair" responses lacking in comparison to the "excellent" responses.

> *MAIN TAKEAWAY*: Treat essay organization and structure as a topic separate from memorization of legal rules. Begin to master essay organization long before you have memorized the legal rules.

PART 1:
HOW TO STRUCTURE YOUR ESSAY

SUMMARY: Use IRAC (Issue, Rules, Application, Conclusion) to structure your essay.

DISCUSSION: Many law school examinations require you to use the "IRAC" method to answer questions. There are myriad variations, such as CRuPAC and CREAC, but in this guide I stick to IRAC because it is the simplest acceptable method, and parsimony is a virtue in a timed, standardized test. Although writing a good IRAC answer is difficult, the specifics of what each letter stands for are quite straightforward.

"I" stands for Issue. You should start each question by identifying the legal issue you have been asked to resolve. **Often, this requires only that you rephrase the question prompt.** For instance, imagine you have been given a Constitutional Law question involving the First Amendment. The first part of the question may ask you if the law in question is "a constitutionally permitted restriction of speech." You should begin your answer by stating that "The issue is whether §12345 of the law in question is a constitutionally permitted restriction of free speech."

"R" stands for Rules. In the Rules section, you need to identify all of the relevant legal rules that you will subsequently use in the Application section of your answer. **Note**: identifying all of the rules you will use is different from identifying every possible relevant legal rule.

You should bring up only those rules you intend to apply in the Application section.

Just as you will lose points for omitting a crucial, relevant rule, you can also drop points for bombarding the grader with irrelevant legal information. In fact, including rules that you do not apply later in the essay is one of the easiest ways to err in the Rules section.

As for what the section should contain, it should look as though you copied and pasted from an outline or from the PowerPoint presentation in your bar review class. Do not get creative and do not try to rewrite the rules in simple English. Avoid colloquialisms and imprecise language. You should just plug in answers from your memory. In other words, the Rules section should read like a flashcard (although it should be a flashcard that uses full sentences).

"A" stands for Application. In this section, you apply the rules you just listed to the facts of the case. Although I, R, and C (discussed below) are simple, A can be complicated. Therefore, I discuss it in detail in Part 4 of this guide.

"C" stands for Conclusion. The Conclusion is a one-to-two-sentence paragraph that gives an answer to the issue you identified in the Issue section. There are literally only three things that can go wrong in this section:

(1) You introduce new legal rules or analysis.

(2) You try so hard to address both sides that you do not answer the question. If you were asked to pick a side, pick a side. (Saying a court will "likely rule" is fine if you feel it is a close issue, but do not tell the grader that the court "could rule in either direction." If the decision could go either way, the grader will be aware of this fact and will award points to essays arguing either conclusion, as long as the legal analysis is sound.)

(3) You run out of time or forget to include the Conclusion section.

MAIN TAKEAWAY: Structure your essay with IRAC. Rephrase the question prompt (Issue), introduce the legal rules you will apply (Rules), apply the rules to the facts (Application), and briefly conclude (Conclusion).

PART 2:
WHAT A PROPER ANSWER LOOKS LIKE VISUALLY

SUMMARY: The four sections of an IRAC answer should have the following lengths:
> (Issue)—short;
> (Rules)—medium;
> (Application)—long;
> (Conclusion)—short.

DISCUSSION: Look at the following model answer to mock MEE question #1. Focus on the layout, rather than the substance. (The question, as well as a discussion of what makes this answer "Excellent", are given in Parts 6 and 7.)

> *The issue is whether Sally is liable to Bill for a breach of contract.*   Issue

> *At common law, an enforceable contract between two parties requires: (1) an offer, (2) an acceptance, and*

(3) consideration. Offers are freely revocable unless there is consideration given to hold an offer open (creating an "option" contract), or there is detrimental reliance on a promise (under a theory of "promissory estoppel"). Compensatory damages for a breach of contract are generally calculated by the amount of money needed to make whole the party that did not breach.

Rules

Here, there was no contract because there was no acceptance. Although Sally made an offer to sell Bill the antique lamp for $100, Bill never actually accepted. He told Sally that it "sounded great," which is ambiguous and could under different circumstances constitute an acceptance, but he then clarified the ambiguity by stating he needed more time to think it over. Therefore, Bill never accepted Sally's offer during their first conversation. He never accepted Sally's offer during their second conversation because, before he could speak, Sally revoked the offer when she told him she had broken the lamp. Although Bill subsequently attempted to accept the offer, the offer was gone.

Application
¶1

Sally was also under no obligation to keep the offer open. Bill never gave Sally anything of value in consideration for her promise to keep the offer open, so no option contract was formed and Sally was not bound by her promise. A theory of promissory estoppel is also unavailable to keep Sally's offer open, because there is no evidence that Bill detrimentally relied on Sally's offer. He researched the value of the lamp and determined it was a good deal, but there is no evidence of reliance.

Application
¶2

If a court somehow erroneously found a breach of contract, it could award $900 in compensatory damages to Bill, because that is the amount of additional money Bill will now need to buy an equivalent lamp. However,

Application
¶3

this is largely irrelevant because a court is exceedingly unlikely to find in Bill's favor.

Therefore, although $900 would be the proper damage award following a determination of breach, Sally will not be found liable to Bill under a theory of breach of contract.　　Conclusion

To illustrate the point about each section's relative length (or brevity), consider the following MEE essay schematic (which should feel very similar to the essay above):

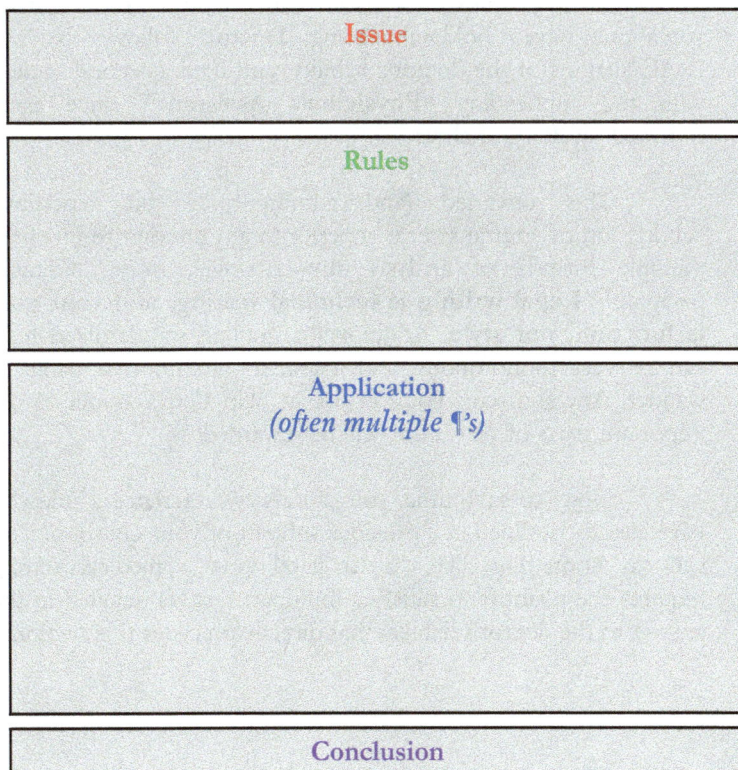

Issue

Rules

Application *(often multiple ¶'s)*

Conclusion

11

In a proper MEE response, there is a short statement of the issue, a medium-length description of the legal rules, a long section applying the law to the facts, and a short conclusion. The Issue and the Conclusion must each be brief, since each is merely a slight variation on the prompt and serves to "frame" the answer. By contrast, there is significant legal substance to the Rules and the Application, so each will be much longer. Finally, the Application will usually be longer than the Rules, since it adds the facts to the legal rules in order to reach a determination of the legal question.

For multipart questions, be sure to use bold headings to delineate each subpart. If one part of a question asks you to evaluate liability issues for a doctor and her physician's assistant, you should have a bold subheading "**Doctor**", followed by your IRAC analysis of the doctor's liability, and then a second section with the subheading "**Physician's Assistant**", once again followed by IRAC analysis.

This unvaried (and admittedly a bit repetitive) subdivision of your answer is superior to any attempt to integrate multiple threads of analysis into a single, more "literary" paragraph. **Legal writing is technical writing, and your goal is function, not style.** Additionally, grading standardized tests can be very monotonous, and a grader's attention is liable to wander. Any shortcuts you can use to help alert a grader to the important parts of your essay will be rewarded!

<u>Note</u>: to save time, you can always reference a rule you have already outlined in a previous subpart of your question. You can say something like, "strict liability in a medical setting requires the plaintiff to satisfy a multipart test, as detailed in the answer to the doctor's liability that directly precedes this section."

MAIN TAKEAWAY: The Issue and Conclusion sections should be short, the Rules section will be medium length, and the Application section may be quite long. Use subheadings liberally to control the organization of multipart questions.

PART 3:
THE INTERNAL SYMMETRY OF AN IRAC ANSWER

> *SUMMARY*: The Conclusion section should mirror the Issue statement, and the Application section should be an expanded mirror (because it incorporates the facts) of your statement of the Rules.

DISCUSSION: You may have noticed heavy repetition in the model answer in Part 2. This is neither a coincidence nor an oversight. There is heavy internal symmetry in a properly written IRAC answer.

All highly structured writing should have elaborate symmetry, and a well-written IRAC essay is no exception. The symmetry between the Issue and the Conclusion is quite straightforward. The Issue statement gives the question the essay will answer, while the Conclusion repeats the answer the essay has provided. The symmetry is self-evident.

The symmetry becomes more interesting and more complicated with respect to the Rules and the Application sections. The Rules section should not be too difficult: you lay out the rules you intend to apply in the Application section in order to reach your Conclusion to the Issue presented. (See how that works? If not, you may want to read through Part 1 again.) But symmetry helps to guide your choice of which rules to include in the Rules section, and which rules to omit.

For instance, you should never include an irrelevant rule in the Rules section. This point seems self-evident. But the technical explanation of why it must be true is slightly more involved:

- The rule is irrelevant only in the sense that it is not needed to answer the issue;

- Consequently, you will not discuss this rule in the Application section;

- Therefore, the rule may not be included in the Rules section, because, due to its omission from the Application section, inclusion in the Rules section would violate the required symmetry between the Rules and the Application sections.

This reasoning gestures at the fundamental relationship between the Rules and the Application sections, which is as follows:

Everything you promise in the Rules you must deliver in the Application.

This relationship means that every rule you present in the Rules section, as well as every legal term you introduce in the Rules section, must correspond to a particular part of the Application section. The rule must reappear in the Application section, augmented by facts, to establish a legal conclusion or an important link to a legal conclusion.

You include the rules you need, and only the rules you need, to meld with the facts, in order to reach a legal conclusion to the issue presented. For instance, avoid the urge to show off how much you have memorized by discoursing on the "majority" rule versus the "minority" rule in the Rules section, unless, in the Application section, you specifically address how this would lead to differing conclusions.

By insisting on perfect "call-and-response" symmetry between your Rules and your Application sections, you can easily determine which rules you need to include, and which you can safely omit. You can also provide a ready structure to your Application section, as will be discussed in Part 4.

MAIN TAKEAWAY: The Application and Rules sections are interconnected. Include in the Rules section every rule you intend to apply in the Application section, and only those rules.

PART 4:
HOW TO STRUCTURE THE "APPLICATION" SECTION OF YOUR ANSWER

SUMMARY: Your Application section integrates key facts from the fact pattern and the rules from your Rules section to reach a legal conclusion. You should avoid both "conclusory reasoning" and "storytelling".

DISCUSSION: When preparing a candidate for the MEE portion of the bar exam, I find that the Application section can be the most challenging part of the process. The Issue, Rules, and Conclusion sections are all, after a little bit of practice, fairly straightforward. This is not the case with the Application section.

The most difficult aspect is the proper use of facts. Many candidates struggle to effectively integrate facts from the fact pattern. Candidates tend to either include too few, which makes the logic of the answer incomplete ("conclusory reasoning"), or they include too many, which makes the Application section a summary of the essay prompt ("storytelling").

"**Conclusory reasoning**" is a term that was used continually throughout my three years of law school, but was never defined in a satisfactory manner. I knew that I was supposed to avoid conclusory reasoning, but it took me a while to figure out precisely what the phrase entailed. Given that it is the easiest way to lose points in the Application section, it is worthwhile to define the term and then examine closely a series of linked examples which illustrate the concept.

<u>Definition</u>: **Conclusory reasoning occurs when a restatement of the conclusion is used as full or partial evidence of the conclusion itself.** In other words, conclusory reasoning occurs when you try to prove a point by paraphrasing the conclusion you hope to reach, rather than by marshaling facts that demonstrate why the conclusion is correct.

<u>Examples and Discussion</u>:

<u>*Prompt*</u>: *"Did the defendant breach the contract?"*

<u>Example #1</u>:

<u>Answer</u>: *"The defendant breached the contract because her behavior after the contract was agreed upon constituted a failure to uphold the terms of the contract that she had agreed to."* **[Conclusory reasoning]**

<u>Discussion</u>: This answer is conclusory because there is no discussion of how or why the defendant breached. The only "evidence" is a restatement that the defendant's behavior did not meet the requirements of performance. This is not evidence; it is the conclusion. Because the reasoning used to reach the conclusion is the conclusion itself, this reasoning is conclusory.

A slightly better response may use a few facts, but it will still be conclusory if the facts are not sufficient to reach the legal conclusion.

Example #2:

Answer: *"The defendant breached the contract because her sale of the computer was contrary to the terms of the contract, and so she failed to uphold the terms of the contract that she had agreed to. This constitutes a breach."* **[Still conclusory reasoning]**

Discussion: Imagine you know nothing about the facts of the case (easy to imagine here, because you do not). This answer is significantly better than answer #1, which told us nothing about what had transpired. We are given some context: apparently the defendant sold a computer and, in so doing, did not fulfill the terms of the contract.

However, we still do not have a full appreciation of what happened, and why exactly there was a breach. We are essentially taking it on faith. **That aspect – being forced to take it on faith – is the essence of conclusory reasoning.** When there is not full evidence of the writer's logical process, we cannot determine for ourselves if the facts merit the conclusion the writer has drawn.

Therefore, because the reasoning leading to the conclusion is, at its core, a mere insistence that the facts are evidence of the conclusion, the reasoning is conclusory.

If you use enough facts to prove to the reader why you reached a certain conclusion, you are no longer guilty of conclusory reasoning.

Example #3:

Answer: *"The defendant breached the contract because her sale of the computer prevented her from bringing the computer to the meeting, as required by the contract. Because the defendant failed to uphold a material term of the contract, she breached."* **[Not conclusory reasoning]**

Discussion: Here we have a full understanding of how and why the defendant breached the contract. She had promised to bring a computer to a meeting, and instead sold the computer and arrived at the meeting without the computer. Because the contract required an action she did not take, she breached the contract. No faith is required to see why the conclusion is merited.

It should be clear at this point that the only way to avoid conclusory reasoning is to use facts. Therefore, the following is the essence of a properly written Application section:

(1) You present key facts from the fact pattern.

(2) You properly situate these facts in the context of the rules you have presented in the Rules section.

(3) You reach a legal conclusion.

These guiding principles lead to the following corollary: **if you fail to use enough facts, it is impossible to avoid conclusory reasoning.**

Although conclusory reasoning is a problem that results from a lack of facts, remember that you can also go overboard by including too many facts. This mistake is called **storytelling**. When you use too many facts, your application section will feel like the introductory paragraph of a persuasive essay, where you are "setting the scene." A telltale sign of too many facts is when you present an entire narrative, rather than gently introduce and summarize a situation. Consider the following example:

Example #4:

Answer: *"On August 1st, the defendant and the plaintiff agreed to a contract. As part of the contract, the defendant promised to bring a computer to the meeting. However, subsequent to the contract's formation but before the meeting, the defendant sold her computer to a third party for a significant sum. The defendant then did not bring a computer to the meeting. Because the defendant failed to uphold a material term of the contract, she breached."* **[Storytelling]**

Discussion: To fix this answer, you need to make an inventory of the facts that are presented in this small passage. Before you go any further, take a minute to determine which are essential and which are superfluous.

*   *   *

See if you agree that the following facts are superfluous:

--"August 1st" (*unnecessary specifics*);

--"subsequent to the contract's formation but before the meeting" (*obvious implications*);

--"third party" (*redundancies*);

--"for a significant sum" (*unnecessary specifics*)

23

Once we strip out the superfluous facts, we are left with the following:

Example #5:

Answer: *"As part of the contract, the defendant had promised to bring a computer to the meeting. When the defendant then sold the computer, and did not bring a computer to the meeting, she failed to uphold a material term of the contract. Consequently, the defendant breached the contract."* **[Neither storytelling nor conclusory reasoning]**

Discussion: It is worth noting that Answer #5 uses more than a third fewer words than did Answer #4 (48 words versus 75 words). While this difference might not seem big, it will add up over the course of a test with a tight time limit.

The three types of facts you can usually remove to improve your answer and avoid storytelling are precisely the three types appearing in Answer #4 on the previous page:

--unnecessary specifics;
--obvious implications;
--redundancies.

You may wonder which of the two "correct" answers (#3 and #5) is preferable. While both are correct, they are stylistically different enough that the best approach is to use a mixture of each technique throughout your examination (or whichever style you feel most comfortable with when under time pressure).

Answer #3 is entirely adequate, and shorter, but it is also very dense. You will struggle to write a readable essay if you consistently cram facts and rules together. On the other hand, Answer #5 has a whiff of repetition to it. For instance, it uses the phrase "bring a computer to the meeting" in two straight sentences. You will likewise struggle to write a readable essay if you are always wordy. The best approach is to try to alternate your rhythm throughout the course of an essay.

A wonderful example that illustrates the importance of alternating sentence structures comes from the late Chief Justice Rehnquist's majority opinion in <u>Calder v. Jones</u>, a case you likely read in first-year Civil Procedure. At one point, there is a particularly boring paragraph, in which Rehnquist summarizes various precedents cited by the Petitioners. He concludes with a sentence that is a full 36 words long (and that is excluding its two full-length citations!). He then starts a new paragraph with the short, punchy line: "Petitioners' analogy does not wash." I still remember the brevity of that sentence, and how this contrast jolted me awake.

A well-written Application section should feel like a sequence of alternating instances of Answers #3 and #5. On each occasion, you take a rule from the Rules section and facts from the fact pattern and combine them to reach a mini-conclusion (in logic, mini-conclusions used on the way to a more complete conclusion are identified by the memorable term "lemmas"). You do this a few times, and your mini-conclusions will combine to answer your Issue statement, at which time you can segue to your Conclusion.

The complexity of the question will determine how many small points you need to stack together to reach your conclusion. For instance, if the rule you gave in the Rules section is a three-part test, you may need three mini-conclusions; however, if one of the three parts of the test is stipulated, then you can mention the stipulation and your Application section will need to reach only two mini-conclusions.

Remember the key to the Application section one last time: **because the facts happened, the rule is met, and therefore the conclusion is achieved**. Facts lead to the rule which leads to the conclusion. You must, must, must use the facts!

> *MAIN TAKEAWAY*: Use facts judiciously in the Application section. If you use too few, you will reach your conclusion without proving it (this is "conclusory reasoning"). If you use too many, you will end up restating the question prompt and distracting from what is essential (this is "storytelling").

PART 5:
SPECIFIC THINGS TO DO (AND TO AVOID)

SUMMARY: The MEE essay is a specific genre of writing. As with all genres, there are particular rules to follow.

DISCUSSION: Here are 5 key "do's" and 5 key "don'ts" to remember for the MEE essay, along with 5 quick reminders from earlier parts of the guide.

- **DO (1): Answer the question, and only the question.**

    Detours are perennial mistakes. You get excited that the question tests material you know well, so you race to write it down. Except...you end up answering a related question, rather than the question that was actually asked.

    For instance, imagine you get a Torts question. You read through the fact pattern and you are ecstatic—it reminds you of a strict liability question you answered for practice a few days before. The question has literally the same facts, and is a straightforward case of strict liability because the activity was inherently dangerous. You start typing and get on a good roll.

27

The only problem is that this question never mentioned strict liability. Instead, it asked: "Will Patricia be able to recover on a negligence theory, and, if so, how much will she recover?" **You did not answer the question**; there is no need to discuss strict liability.

This seems like an obvious pitfall to avoid, and it is, but many people still make the mistake (and not just on the bar exam!). Be aware, and make sure you avoid the trap.

- **DO (2): Spend 2-3 minutes outlining your answer before you start writing.**

This technique is an excellent way to avoid the trap of answering the wrong question. It is also a good policy in general.

When you first see the question, all sorts of thoughts will rush through your head. For instance, you may think of something that bears mentioning in the second half of the question. Unfortunately, there is no way you will still remember this point in 15 minutes, when you actually get to the second half of the question. Few people are lucky enough to think of the things they wish to mention in the order they should be mentioned, so a quick outline of key points can be immensely helpful.

Another advantage of outlining is that it helps you to avoid conclusory reasoning. This is true because, when you outline, you are forced to engage with the facts. An easy way to slip into conclusory reasoning is to write the Application section without knowing which facts you want to use. When you are uncertain, you may not use the facts as much as you should, which can lead to conclusory reasoning. Therefore, as you outline, be sure to note which facts you think will be crucial for the Application section.

HOW TO WRITE BAR EXAM MEE ESSAYS

I have never had a student who doubted that outlining was useful. The major pushback is that, with only 30 minutes per MEE essay, it takes too much time. Spending too much time on the outline is a real concern, which is why you should limit your outlining to 2-3 minutes per question. If you also take 2-3 minutes to read the fact pattern, this will leave you with about 25 minutes to write each essay, which is the sweet spot for using your time efficiently.

- **DO (3): Use transition words and phrases.**

Transition words and phrases are at a premium because a grader needs to be able to track your logic and see what you are thinking. Using words like "therefore", "however", "consequently", and "nevertheless" allows the reader to understand where you are in your reasoning. The better the reader is able to follow what you are thinking, the more likely you are to receive a high score.

I think transition words and phrases sometimes get a bad reputation because they can feel stiff and make writing seem reductionist. In many circumstances, this criticism is warranted, but legal writing is not one of these situations. **In legal writing, your goal should be clarity**, even if it comes at the expense of the quality of your prose. Therefore, you should use transition words and phrases.

(N.B. Boring writing is not a virtue in and of itself. It is easy to be both boring and opaque. Just make sure you never choose flair over clarity on your MEE essays, if you feel you are forced to choose.)

- **DO (4): Memorize precise definitions for common rules.**

Some topics come up more frequently than other topics. Product liability may or may not be part of a Torts question, but hearsay shows up in at least some part of almost every Evidence question. There is no excuse not to have memorized the rules associated with these frequently-tested topics, all the way down to the last comma.

A few obvious topics, for which you should have precise definitions of the related rules, include (but are very much not limited to):

- o <u>Contracts</u>: consideration; contract formation
- o <u>Corporations</u>: fiduciary duties
- o <u>Evidence</u>: hearsay; Miranda rights
- o <u>Property</u>: assignment and sublease
- o <u>Torts</u>: negligence; strict liability

Obviously, you should memorize as much legal material as you can; that goes without saying. The point here is that there are a handful of topics that appear so frequently, year after year, that the optimal use of your study time is to memorize, word-for-word, a perfect definition for all of the associated rules. It is one thing to have to paraphrase a Secured Transactions rule that just so happens to appear on your MEE exam, but it is an avoidable moment of stress if you find yourself scrambling to find the right wording for hearsay.

You <u>must</u> commit these most frequently tested rules to memory.

HOW TO WRITE BAR EXAM MEE ESSAYS

- **DO (5): Know what topics are likely to be tested.**

The National Council of Bar Examiners (NCBE) lists 12 possible MEE essay topics on its website:

- o Business Associations
- o Civil Procedure
- o Conflict of Laws
- o Constitutional Law
- o Contracts
- o Criminal Law and Procedure
- o Evidence
- o Family Law
- o Property
- o Secured Transactions
- o Torts
- o Trusts and Estates

However, not every topic is tested with equal frequency. For instance, over the past ten years, Business Associations and Civil Procedure have been tested on almost every exam, whereas Conflict of Laws has occurred only occasionally.

Additionally, it has historically been the case that a topic is significantly more likely to be on any given MEE if it was omitted from the preceding MEE. Although this phenomenon has lessened somewhat in the past few years, it still appears to be the case that a topic is more likely to show up on the current exam if it did not appear on the previous administration of the exam.

Therefore, you should study a little bit harder for both: (i) the perennial essay topics that are on most exams (like Civil Procedure), as well as (ii) any essay topics that were <u>not</u> on the most recent bar exam.

- **DON'T (1): Don't make a policy argument.**

Your answers will be read by practitioners, not professors. In contrast to law school, where theory is important, the bar exam does not require you to have an opinion on why the law is the way it is. You simply need to know what the law is, and how it applies to the facts.

Additionally, grading policy arguments would be unmanageable on the bar exam, because it would be too discretionary. Bar exam graders grade from a rubric to ensure uniformity. Evaluating the quality of a policy argument would be beyond the scope of what could be done easily and consistently across thousands of essays.

Policy arguments are dead ends, so you should avoid them on the bar exam.

- **DON'T (2): Don't jeopardize the accuracy of your analysis by trying too hard to sound sophisticated and using the wrong terms.**

Sometimes candidates try too hard to sound official or sophisticated. They want to impress their graders by showing them how much they have learned in law school. This can manifest itself in word choice. However, legal vocabulary is a really important part of the bar exam. Candidates sometimes err by substituting a more complicated legal word or phrase for a simpler word or phrase, when the two are related but are not synonyms.

The choice of a single word can dramatically change the complexion of an answer. For instance, consider the difference between an argument that involves "increasing damages" and another that involves "increasing injury". Injury and damages, although closely related, are different concepts and should not be used interchangeably.

Similar examples abound: scope of duty is not the same as one's scope of employment; a benefactor is not a beneficiary. The opportunities to run into trouble with loose word choices are endless. Be very careful that you use the words you intend, rather than the words that you think sound the best.

- **DON'T (3): Don't go to extreme lengths to save time.**

When test takers fear that they may run out of time, they sometimes lapse into poor habits. One such example is substituting P and D for plaintiff and defendant. A related slip-up would be using the first initials of names, such as A and B, for Alice and Ben.

Anything you do that interrupts the visual rhythm of an answer is a bad idea. Single letters can disappear into the many lines of text you have produced, and graders are prone to miss them. Additionally, graders may become confused when the names presented in the fact pattern are not used. It is not their job to decipher your naming conventions; it is your job to make their lives easy. For the two seconds you might save, it is not worth the risk.

Another instance of unwise abbreviations is when you start citing cases to save time in the Rules section. Do not say, "The <u>Vosburg</u> rule means the defendant is liable for all the damages." Explain what the rule is (and there is no need to cite the case, such as <u>Vosburg</u>, that created the rule), and what it means for the defendant's liability.

Time can be a huge issue, but do not use time as a justification to use abbreviations or shortcuts. **Manage your time so that you can go into detail and earn full points.**

- **DON'T (4): Don't deviate from your time budget.**

Although you should not cut corners to save time, you must stay on schedule with the MEE. If you systematically 'borrow' a few minutes on each essay early in the exam, you may very well end up in the unenviable situation of having something like 18 minutes left to write your final essay.

It is almost impossible to write a high-scoring essay in substantially less than the 30 minutes you are allotted. As difficult as it may seem, you need to adhere strictly to your time budget, or your score will suffer. Going 45 seconds over your budgeted time to finish a sentence or make sure you have a conclusion is fine, but repeatedly 'borrowing' time will have unfortunate ramifications for the final few essays.

- **DON'T (5): Don't panic and leave the section blank when you forget something.**

It is inevitable, or at least very likely, that at some point in the MEE essay exam you will forget something. The worst thing you can do when you forget something is to leave the entire section blank.

Even if you get the rule wrong, you need to put something down in the Rules section. Without any rule, you will inevitably get zero points in your Application section, too, because there is no rule to apply. However, if you have put down a rule that is at least similar to the proper rule, you can then proceed to perform your analysis. And, if you use the facts properly and structure your Application section as you should, you can still get a few points, even if your Rules section turns out to be incorrect.

It is very possible to get a few points even if you do not have a great grasp of what is happening in an MEE essay. You will be rewarded for structure and thoroughness. Especially on more obscure subjects that are tested less frequently and are not on the MBE, it can be difficult to have every rule memorized. In these cases, make sure you put something down, so you can write the whole essay and salvage some points.

REMINDER #1: You can usually argue either way on a question, but you should **never argue both ways. Pick a side** and support it with rules and facts.

REMINDER #2: **Avoid conclusory reasoning**. Do not say "the facts do not support the polo shirt part of the test." Instead, say that "the test is not met because the defendant was not wearing a polo shirt at the time when it was required."

REMINDER #3: **Never bring up a new rule or test in the** Application **section**, and do not bring up any tests in the Rules section that you do not apply in the Application section. All rules and tests should be in both sections, or they should be in neither section.

REMINDER #4: **Don't assume there is only one area of law being tested**—the MEE can throw in a second, related subject. This situation often occurs with Choice of Law, but can occur elsewhere, too, such as with Wills & Trusts and Family Law.

REMINDER #5: **Remember to outline and pace yourself.** Many candidates jump to the Application section too quickly, thinking that is all that matters. Remember that Issue, Rules and Conclusion are, taken together, worth a very large number of points.

PART 6:
SIMPLIFIED MOCK MEE: QUESTIONS

Throughout this guide, I refer to the essays from the simplified mock MEE on the next two pages. These questions differ from real MEE questions mostly in the respect that they have only one part, rather than multiple, related questions. Working with shorter examples simplifies the process of learning to write an MEE essay, but you should be aware that real MEE essays may often be more complicated.

Actual MEE essays from the past few years, along with excellent model answers, are available for free on several state board of bar examiner websites. In the past, I have used materials from the website of the New York State Board of Law Examiners (https://www.nybarexam.org). I like the New York site because the model answers they provide are high quality answers that you could reasonably hope to approximate under test conditions, rather than the 99th percentile answers of examinees who were clearly over-prepared for that specific question.

Try your hand at these two questions before proceeding to Part 7. As I discussed in the introduction, it is fine to peek at your Torts and Contracts outlines if you forget any of the legal rules you feel you need to answer these questions.

Mock MEE Question #1 – Contracts:

Bill needed to buy a lamp. He asked his friend Sally, who had lots of furniture, if she had an extra lamp she would sell him.

Sally offered to sell Bill an antique lamp for $100. Bill told Sally, "That sounds great. I need some time to think it over; please keep the offer open for me." Sally told Bill she would hold the offer open to him for one week. Bill thanked her and headed to the local furniture store to research lamps.

Six days later, Bill decided that he would accept Sally's offer. Just then, he was surprised when the phone rang. It was Sally. She informed him that she had dropped the lamp and broken it. "I'm sorry, but I guess the offer is gone now!" she told him. Bill protested that she was bound to keep the offer open, and that he was going to accept it. (He had learned at the furniture store that a lamp like the one Sally owned could cost $1000.)

Bill is now threatening to sue Sally for $900. This is a common law jurisdiction. Evaluate his contract claim.

Mock MEE Question #2 - Torts:

Dave is driving his friend Patricia to the beach on a beautiful summer day. Dave is usually an excellent driver. He is going exactly at the speed limit of 65 miles per hour.

When they are halfway there, it starts to rain. The rain becomes torrential and visibility becomes quite poor. Dave slows down to 60 miles per hour to account for the rain.

They arrive at the beach and the rain stops. They have a wonderful day at the beach. On the drive home, Patricia tells Dave, "That was scary on the way here. The next time there is heavy rain, would you please slow down even more?" Dave tells Patricia that he will.

On the way home, Dave is once again traveling at exactly the speed limit of 65 miles per hour. When they are halfway home, a sudden rainstorm appears once again. This time, Dave slows down from 65 to 55 miles per hour, because the visibility is horrible and the rain is blinding.

After a few minutes of driving in the storm, a tractor-trailer truck skids and strikes Dave and Patricia's car. They flip over, and although Dave is unscathed, Patricia suffers serious injuries that require extensive surgeries and a prolonged hospitalization. She eventually receives a $100,000 medical bill. She also misses eight weeks of her job that pays her $1,000 per week.

Patricia wants to sue Dave for $108,000. This is a common law jurisdiction. Will she be able to recover on a negligence theory, and, if so, how much will she recover?

PART 7:
SIMPLIFIED MOCK MEE: MODEL ANSWERS AND COMMENTARY

SUMMARY**:** For each essay, I give an "Excellent" response and a "Fair" response. I also explain what the issues are with the answers which are merely "Fair."

DISCUSSION**:** In this Part of the guide, I present four graded essays from the simplified mock exam given in Part 6. For each of the two questions, I provide an "Excellent" response (which I would grade at either a 5 or a 6 on a scale of 1-to-6 possible points), and a "Fair" response (which I would grade at either 2 or 3 points out of 6).

(Note: different states use different grading scales. Some grade essays out of 6 possible points, others out of 10 points, and New York even uses a scale from 20-80. You should familiarize yourself with your jurisdiction's scale. I use a scale of 1-6 because the National Conference of Bar Examiners uses a 1-6 scale in its internal grading workshop, as discussed in a past edition of The

Bar Examiner periodical. Of course, the number of points at the top end of a grading scale has no effect on the grading criteria.)

Crucially, I want to emphasize that there is nothing specifically incorrect with the "Fair" responses to the two mock MEE questions reproduced in this Part of the guide. It would not help you if I presented an unequivocally bad essay with misstated legal rules and incoherent analysis. Instead, the problems with these responses, and the reason they do not score well, stem from three things: (1) poor organization, (2) important omissions, and (3) inclusions of extraneous material. They are well-written and do nothing a non-lawyer would recognize as "wrong."

Every divergence between the "Excellent" response and the "Fair" response is marked by a footnote in the "Fair" response. These notes are discussed after both essays are presented. (Note that the answers are presented side-by-side to facilitate comparison. **An actual response should never have the large, mid-answer white spaces that this presentation creates.**)

Question #1 – Contracts: "Excellent" Response:

The issue is whether Sally is liable to Bill for a breach of contract.

At common law, an enforceable contract between two parties requires: (1) an offer, (2) an acceptance, and (3) consideration.

Offers are freely revocable unless there is consideration given to hold an offer open (creating an "option" contract), or there is detrimental reliance on a promise (under a theory of "promissory estoppel"). Compensatory damages for a breach of contract are generally calculated by the amount of money needed to make whole the party that did not breach.

Here, there was no contract because there was no acceptance. Although Sally made an offer to sell Bill the antique lamp for $100, Bill

Question #1 – Contracts: "Fair" Response:

[1]At common law, an enforceable contract between two parties requires: (1) an offer, (2) an acceptance, and (3) consideration. The two parties must assent to the same thing, sometimes called a "meeting of the minds."[2] Offers are freely revocable unless there is consideration given to hold an offer open (creating an "option" contract).[3]

Compensatory damages for a breach of contract are generally calculated by the amount of money needed to make whole the party that did not breach.

Here, there was no contract because there was no acceptance.

never actually accepted. He told Sally that it "sounded great," which is ambiguous and could under different circumstances constitute an acceptance, but he then clarified the ambiguity by stating he needed more time to think it over. Therefore, Bill never accepted Sally's offer during their first conversation. He never accepted Sally's offer during their second conversation because, before he could speak, Sally revoked the offer when she told him she had broken the lamp. Although Bill subsequently attempted to accept the offer, the offer was gone.

Bill never accepted Sally's offer during their first conversation. He never accepted Sally's offer during their second conversation.[4]

There was also no "meeting of the minds."[5]

Sally was also under no obligation to keep the offer open. Bill never gave Sally anything of value in consideration for her promise to keep the offer open, so no option contract was formed and Sally was not bound by her promise. A theory of promissory estoppel is also unavailable to keep Sally's offer open, because there is no evidence that Bill

Sally was also under no obligation to keep the offer open. Bill never gave Sally anything of value in consideration for her promise to keep the offer open, so no option contract was formed and Sally was not bound by her promise. A theory of promissory estoppel is also unavailable to keep Sally's offer open, because there is no evidence that Bill

44

detrimentally relied on Sally's offer. He researched the value of the lamp and determined it was a good deal, but there is no evidence of reliance.

If a court somehow erroneously found a breach of contract, it could award $900 in compensatory damages to Bill, because that is the amount of additional money Bill will now need to buy an equivalent lamp. However, this is largely irrelevant because a court is exceedingly unlikely to find in Bill's favor.

Therefore, although $900 would be the proper damage award following a determination of breach, Sally will not be found liable to Bill under a theory of breach of contract.

detrimentally relied on Sally's offer. He researched the value of the lamp and determined it was a good deal, but there is no evidence of reliance.[6]

If a court somehow erroneously found a breach of contract, it could award $900 in compensatory damages to Bill.[7]

However, this is largely irrelevant because a court is exceedingly unlikely to find in Bill's favor.

Therefore, although $900 would be the proper damage award following a determination of breach, Sally will not be found liable to Bill under a theory of breach of contract.

Discussion of the flaws in the "Fair" response:

- *Note #1*: This essay is missing a statement of the issue.

- *Note #2*: There is a superfluous reference to the concept of a "meeting of the minds." This definition is correct, and the concept is relevant for many Contract questions. However, the concept is irrelevant to the issue presented, and its use does not contribute to the essay's logical progression. It should be omitted from this answer.

- *Note #3*: The reference to the concept of promissory estoppel is missing from the Rules section. Promissory estoppel and "option" contract are the two theories available to keep the offer open, so both should be addressed. Furthermore, although it is not the end of the world to omit discussion of promissory estoppel ("option" contract is the more likely theory given the fact pattern), promissory estoppel is addressed in the Application section, so its omission in the Rules section violates the requirement of symmetry between Rules and Application.

- *Note #4*: The thorough reasoning of the "Excellent" essay has been replaced by conclusory reasoning in the "Fair" essay. All of the facts have been omitted (Sally made an offer, Bill told her it "sounded great", Bill asked for more time to think it over, Sally revoked the offer by telling him she broke the lamp), and they have been replaced by the conclusions drawn from them.

- *Note #5*: There is a passing reference to a "meeting of the minds". This is good in the sense that it was necessary (due to its inclusion in the "Fair" response's Rules section), but once again, the reasoning is conclusory. There is also no explanation of why this reference is relevant to the issue of contract formation (it is not, in fact, relevant).

- *Note #6*: The discussion of promissory estoppel is the same as in the "Excellent" response. However, the problem is that, in the "Fair" essay, there was no reference to promissory estoppel in the Rules section (see Note #3); therefore, there should be no discussion of promissory estoppel in the Application section.

- _Note #7_: There is no explanation for how the $900 figure was determined. Note that this is not an example of conclusory reasoning, because there is no reasoning. It is simply a restatement.

Any one of these errors is a small-to-middling problem in isolation. I purposely chose not to commit any significant errors, because an obviously bad essay is not instructive. However, the entirety of the errors results in an essay that is fundamentally underdeveloped, and its score will suffer accordingly.

Question #2 – Torts: "Excellent" Response:

The issue is whether Dave has been negligent, and if he is therefore liable to Patricia.

Liability for negligence requires a demonstration of: (1) duty, (2) breach, (3) causation and (4) damages. First, a plaintiff must show that the defendant owed her a duty of care. Second, should the duty exist, if the defendant fails to exercise this duty, it would constitute a breach. Third, to show causation, a plaintiff must show that the defendant's actions were both the "but for" and the "proximate" causes of the injury. "But for" causation requires a demonstration that the injury would not have occurred without the defendant's breach; "proximate" causation requires a showing that the injury was a foreseeable result of the plaintiff's breach. Finally, the plaintiff must prove that the breach caused her damages.

Question #2 – Torts: "Fair" Response:

The issue is whether Dave has been negligent, and if he is therefore liable to Patricia.

Liability for negligence requires a demonstration of: (1) duty, (2) breach, (3) causation and (4) damages.[1]

In this case, Patricia can demonstrate that Dave owed her a duty. Dave owed Patricia the general duty of care to act as a reasonably prudent person. Since Dave was the driver of a car in which Patricia was a passenger, in this instance the general duty of care required him to drive in the manner of a reasonably prudent person. Next, Patricia needs to demonstrate that Dave breached this duty. Although Dave is usually an excellent driver and he never exceeded the speed limit, driving within the speed limit is not dispositive proof that Dave complied with his duty of care. On the other hand, Patricia's requests that Dave drive slowly also do not affect whether or not Dave breached, because asking someone to drive safely does not modify the requirements to fulfill a general duty of care. Ultimately, a finder of fact would likely find that Dave breached his duty of care, because 55 miles per hour in a 65 mile per hour zone is still traveling too quickly when the road

In this case, Patricia can demonstrate that Dave owed her a duty. Dave owed Patricia the general duty of care.[2]

Next, Patricia needs to demonstrate that Dave breached this duty.

Ultimately, a finder of fact would likely find that Dave breached his duty of care, because 55 miles per hour in a 65 mile per hour zone is still traveling too quickly when the road conditions are so poor that there is almost no visibility and the rain is "blinding."

Patricia's claim will founder, however, with regard to causation. She can easily demonstrate "proximate" causation, because a car crash is exactly the sort of foreseeable harm that is likely to occur when you drive too quickly in a rainstorm. It is with respect to "but for" causation that Patricia's claim will fail. Patricia was injured when Dave's car flipped over, but Dave's car did not flip over due to Dave's driving. The car flipped over because it was struck by a skidding tractor-trailer truck. Given the poor visibility, it is unlikely that Dave would have been able to avoid the skidding truck, even if he had been driving more slowly. In fact, being struck by a skidding truck seems like precisely the sort of bad-luck accident that no amount of prudence could prevent (other than by not driving at all). Therefore, although Dave breached his duty of care, his breach was not the "but for" cause of

conditions are so poor that there is almost no visibility and the rain is "blinding."[3]

Patricia's claim will founder, however, with regard to causation. She can easily demonstrate "proximate" causation, because a car crash is exactly the sort of foreseeable harm that is likely to occur when you drive too quickly in a rainstorm. It is with respect to "but for" causation that Patricia's claim will fail.

In fact, being struck by a skidding truck seems like precisely the sort of bad-luck accident that no amount of prudence could prevent (other than by not driving at all).[4] Therefore, although Dave breached his duty of care, his breach was not the "but for" cause of

Patricia's injuries. Even if he had driven more safely, she would have still been injured.

If a court were to find causation, Patricia would have no trouble proving damages as the fourth and final part of her negligence claim. She suffered $108,000 of damages: $100,000 due to her hospital bill, and $8,000 due to her 8 weeks of lost wages. Because she is not seeking punitive damages or pain and suffering, she would receive exactly the $108,000 in damages that she is seeking.

Nonetheless, Dave will not owe Patricia anything, as he is not likely to be found liable on a negligence theory. The negligence theory will fail on the causation element, because Dave's breach was not the "but for" cause of Patricia's injury.

Patricia's injuries. Even if he had driven more safely, she would have still been injured.

If a court were to find causation, Patricia would have no trouble proving damages as the fourth and final part of her negligence claim. She suffered $108,000 of damages: $100,000 due to her hospital bill, and $8,000 due to her 8 weeks of lost wages. Because she is not seeking punitive damages or pain and suffering, she would receive exactly the $108,000 in damages that she is seeking.

Nonetheless, Dave will not owe Patricia anything, as he is not likely to be found liable on a negligence theory. The negligence theory will fail on the causation element, because Dave's breach was not the "but for" cause of Patricia's injury.[5]

However, Patricia may be able to succeed on a theory of strict liability. Strict liability will apply if an activity is deemed "inherently dangerous." Although driving is not an inherently dangerous

51

activity, Patricia may be able to convince a court that driving in the blinding rain is an inherently dangerous activity, because no amount of care can make it safe. The facts of the case bear this conclusion out exactly: Dave appeared to conform to the driving of a reasonably prudent person, and yet his car was struck unexpectedly by a skidding truck.

Therefore, if Patricia is able to convince the court that driving in the blinding rain is inherently dangerous, she may be able to recover on a theory of strict liability.[6]

Discussion of the flaws in the "Fair" Response:

- *Note #1*: The Rules section is too short. Although it contains the correct four-part test for negligence, the four parts must be explained in more detail.

- *Note #2*: The description of what the duty of care is in this instance (the "reasonably prudent person" standard of the general duty of care) should not have been omitted.

- *Note #3*: The reasoning in this passage is not conclusory reasoning (there are some facts given which justify the conclusion), but the reasoning is nonetheless too shallow and the analysis does not use all of the facts that it could. There should be a discussion of the speed limit and Patricia's requests that Dave drive more slowly, and how these affect (or do not affect) potential breach of duty.

- *Note #4*: This passage is flawed because it demonstrates conclusory reasoning: the recitation of only a few facts is insufficient to justify the conclusion. There should be a discussion that the injury occurred when the car flipped over and that the car flipped over when it was struck by the truck. (Such a discussion is present in the "Excellent" response.)

- *Note #5*: This is not a mistake, but a point of emphasis. **In many questions, this one included, there is not a "correct answer" with respect to the legal conclusion** of whether Dave was (or was not) negligent. Although the Contracts question had only one correct response, this Torts question was written in a way such that reasonable minds could disagree and still earn (close to) full points. A well-written answer that argued "but for" causation had been met – because of an argument that Dave may have been able to avoid the truck, or at least mitigate the damage from a collision, if he were driving much slower – would score very well, even if that argument does seem a little stretched based on the facts.

- *Note #6*: This discussion is an excellent, compact discussion of strict liability. All four IRAC sections are given in the span of a single paragraph. But the question only asked for a discussion of negligence, so this section on strict liability is superfluous. You will not get any points if you go on a tangent, even if the tangent is thoughtful and the analysis is accurate.

Conclusion:
Finding Success with MEE Essays

> **SUMMARY**: Do not wait until the last few weeks before the exam to learn how to structure your bar exam essays. Acknowledge that structuring and organizing essays is a distinct skill that must be acquired with repeated practice.

DISCUSSION: Succeeding on the MEE part of the bar exam requires two things. First, you need to know the underlying legal material. To do so is time consuming but straightforward: you can learn this through diligent application in your bar exam review course (especially since it overlaps a great deal with your preparation for the MBE).

The second requirement for success can be trickier to acquire, and it is the subject of this Guide. **To succeed on the MEE requires an understanding of how to structure a bar exam essay.** It is critical to your development of this skill that you start early. If you wait until you have finally learned the underlying legal material, you may find yourself with very little time in which to learn how to organize your MEE essays.

Start the process of learning how to structure your MEE essays at the beginning of your bar exam preparation, not the end. Look up the rules you do not know to simulate what it will feel like when you eventually have them committed to memory. This way, you can learn how to write your essays without waiting until the last few weeks before the exam.

The bar exam can be scary and overwhelming, but you can master it by breaking it down into its component parts. **You need to realize that writing essays is a skill, not a talent, and it is a skill that can be acquired by repeated, focused practice**—even if you have yet to memorize the legal rules.

<u>Try to write two essays each day of your bar exam review period</u>. This corresponds to an hour of work, and it will be time well spent. By the time the MEE day of the bar exam rolls around, you will be comfortable writing concise, IRAC-structured essays in the 30 minutes you are allotted.

Good luck!

HOW TO WRITE BAR EXAM MEE ESSAYS

ABOUT THE AUTHOR

Alexander Marcus is an educator, author, and retired attorney.
Over the past twenty years, he has worked with students and
families to help turn educational dreams into realities.

My Notes:

My Notes:

My Notes:

My Notes:

HOW TO WRITE BAR EXAM MEE ESSAYS

www.ingramcontent.com/pod-product-compliance
Lightning Source LLC
Chambersburg PA
CBHW060157070426
42447CB00033B/2196